# Story Cards: Aesop's Fables

Compiled by

Raymond C. Clark

with illustrations by

Hannah Bonner

PRO LINGUA ASSOCIATES

Brattleboro, Vermont

**Pro Lingua Associates, Publishers**
**15 Elm Street**
**Brattleboro, Vermont 05301 USA**

Office 802-257-7779
Orders 800-366-4775
San 216-0579

**At Pro Lingua,**
our objective is to foster an approach
to learning and teaching that we call
**interplay**, the **inter**action of language
learners and teachers with their materials,
with the language and culture,
and with each other in active, creative,
and productive **play.**

Copyright © 1995 by Raymond C. Clark
ISBN 0-86647-086-7
All rights reserved. No part of this publication may be reproduced or transmitted in any form or by any means, electronic, mechanical, photocopying, recording, or other, or stored in an information storage or retrieval system without permission in writing from the pubisher.

This book was designed and set by Arthur A. Burrows using Century Schoolbook type with Zapf Chancery display type and printed and bound by BookCrafters of Chelsea, Michigan.

This edition is published by arrangement with Pro Lingua Associates. Neither this book nor any part thereof may be reproduced by any process whatsoever without the written permission of Foreign Language Limited and Pro Lingua Associates.
**First Korean edition** printed in South Korea in 1997: **ISBN** 89-86159-18-X 13740

# How to Prepare Your Story Cards

These Story Cards come in sheets of four, bound together as a book for ease of handling and to save you money. To prepare the cards for use, follow these easy steps.

**1.** Tear the pages of cards out of the book; they are perforated at the spine. Cut each sheet in four along the dotted line, trimming the rough edge.

**2.** These cards are on tough coated stock, but they will last longer if you laminate them.

**3.** Keep this introductory material in a file for future reference.

# Contents

# Who was Aesop?

Aesop is a legendary figure. Maybe he was a real person who created the fable for western literature, and maybe he created and told many of the fables in this collection. Maybe Aesop was created as a mythical storyteller who specialized in fables.

There are some legends about Aesop. If he lived, he probably lived about 2,500 years ago, in the 6th century B.C. He may have been born in Thrace (northern Greece). One legend says that he was a slave and lived on the island of Samos in the Aegean Sea.

There is no evidence that a person named Aesop actually wrote anything, but he may have been simply a well-known storyteller who never bothered to write anything. It may be that his fables were passed down orally from generation to generation in true folk tradition. It is known, however, that a collection of stories ascribed to Aesop was published in the 4th century B.C. This collection has been lost, but it may have been the basis for a later collection written in Latin by a Roman writer, Phaedrus, in the 1st century A.D. Another, later collection was written in Greek by Babrius in the 2nd century A.D. These two works were influential in establishing the fable as a story form. They were probably the inspiration for the French fabulist La Fontaine who popularized the fable for the western world in the 17th century.

# Teaching Notes

The fable seems to be almost a universal art form, suggesting that it is a natural expression of the human experience. The fable is essentially a moral lesson that one generation uses to teach the next, and typically the lesson features animals, possibly because animals have always fascinated young children, the object of the lesson.

Fables, however, are not just stories for children. They are remembered and quoted by adults. They can be a simple and amusing explanation of why things go wrong in the adult world, and they are often an ironic comment on the weaknesses — and the strengths — of the human race. Many of them, with their short, pithy morals have become fixtures in the language as proverbs and idioms. For example, most speakers of English are well acquainted with the idiom "sour grapes" (See "The Fox and the Grapes") and the proverb "Slow and steady wins the race" (See "The Tortoise and the Hare").

In short, fables are very useful cultural statements that have universality and at the same time cultural specificity.

## What are these *Story Cards* for?

The basic purpose of this collection is really quite simple. Storytelling is an excellent way for language learners to practice the language they are learning in a holistic way, building fluency, confidence, and communicative competence as well as gaining insight into the cultural values and norms underlying the language.

There are 48 cards in this collection, and on each card is a short fable in clear, modified English. The cards are numbered and, with the exception of the first fable, are ordered from short and easy to longer and more difficult. They can be used by a range of learners, from beginning level to advanced.

The very first card in this collection, "Aesop and the Athenian," may serve as an introduction to the collection and its use in the classroom. We invite you to begin your exploration of the fables by telling this fable to the class and then leading them in a discussion about Aesop, the fable's meaning and the creation of a moral or a saying such as, "All work and no play .........."

This collection of fables on cards is not intended as a primary way to teach *new* material to learners. The purpose is to stimulate speaking practice, to provide listening practice, and to offer some reading practice. However, it is likely that some new vocabulary will be learned, and some grammatical features can be highlighted. But as these are not primary purposes of these cards, practice exercises are notably absent. Telling a story should be primarily a synthesizing activity, and fun.

### 1. *The basic technique.*

It is quite simple. Give each student in the class a different card. Have them read through the cards silently for comprehension. Circulate and answer questions. Some words may emerge as unknown but necessary to the successful telling of the fable. Take a few minutes to put these words on the board and make sure everybody knows the meaning. With the potentially troublesome vocabulary out of the way, pair the students and have them tell each other their stories. Encourage them to look again at their stories after they have told them, to compare their auditory short-term memory with the story as it is told on the card. They can also show their cards to each other for a brief follow-up reading practice. Then the pair splits up and they find someone else to share stories with. This continues as many times as you want, although the activity may wear thin after eight exchanges.

There are variations on this technique and other activities that can be done with the cards. A few are suggested below.

### 2. *Chain Stories.*

Arrange the students in a circle. An even number of students works best. Give a different card to every other student in the circle. The students with the cards tell their fables to the students to their left who are without cards. Then the students who listened turn to the next student in the circle and tell that person the fable, and so on. After all the fables have been told, compare the final versions with the original versions on the card.

A variation on this technique is to send a few students out of the room. Bring them in one at a time. Someone in the room tells a fable to the student who comes in. That student tells the fable to the next student who comes in, and so on. Again, compare the final version with the original.

3. *Dictation.*

Dictate a fable to the students, or have pairs of students dictate fables to each other. This is good practice for the punctuation of direct speech.

4. *Discussion.*

Have the class try to produce a simple, one sentence moral for the fable. They can also talk about personal experiences that exemplify the moral. They may also have similar fables from their own cultural tradition that can be compared to the original.

5. *Listen and Write.*

Read a fable to the students, and then have them write it out. After they have written it, read it again and let them compare. They can also swap their writings and compare.

6. *Act it out.*

Give a fable to a group of students (one student for each character in the fable plus a narrator) and have them act it out for their classmates.

7. *For the Record.*

After practicing several times, the students take turns making audio or video recordings of their storytelling. Play the tape for the class and for another class, if possible. This activity can be repeated later in the course. By comparing the two tapes, the students should be able to see their progress.

8. *Information Gap Practice.*

Make two enlarged copies of the same fable for each pair of students. White-out two different sets of words on the two cards (six to ten blanks are usually enough). One student in each pair reads while the other listens. The readers begin reading their cards, pausing when they come to a missing word. The listeners supply the words and at the same time try to fill in the words that are missing on their own cards. *(Permission is given to photocopy for this kind of activity).*

## Who are these cards designed for?

Anyone studying language arts or English as a second or foreign language will benefit from telling, listening to, reading, and writing these fables. Students with third grade reading skills or advanced beginner language proficiency will be able to use at least the shorter, easier fables. Although the stories will have great appeal to children, adults also will enjoy language learning with the fables.

## How many students can use one set of cards?

These cards can be used in a tutorial situation. They are very effective for pair work activities. They can also be used by large classes, although it is best to have a set of cards for each eight to ten students because this will allow you to use the activity several times with your class. Thus, you can have sub-groups each working with a complete set of cards.

## Using two sets of cards

There are advantages to having two sets of cards, even with a small class *(Photocopying for this purpose is not permitted).* Two students can work as a pair with the same fable. They can practice telling it to each other, mutually monitoring and prompting each other. They can focus on accuracy as well as fluency. This could be a very good way of preparing for *The Basic Technique* (#1), described above. In short, two students practice the same fable together and then split up to tell their fable to others, and so on.

## The art of storytelling

In the last few years there has been increasing interest in the art of storytelling. It is an art form that can be developed easily and naturally if it is encouraged. These story cards can provide an ideal vehicle for developing your students' storytelling skills along with increasing their confidence and fluency. We encourage you, the teacher, to model some of these fables or other stories, using your best dramatic and expressive skills.

## Other **Story Card** collections available

Pro Lingua Associates has two other collections of these **Story Cards.** They are **North American Indian Tales** by Susannah J. Clark, with illustrations by Ken Rainbow Cougar Edwards, and **Tales of Nasreddin Hodja** also by Raymond C. Clark, with illustrations by Robert MacLean.

# The Fox and the Grapes

STORY CARDS: AESOP'S FABLES
*compiled by Raymond C. Clark, illustrated by Hannah Bonner*
PRO LINGUA ASSOCIATES
15 Elm Street, Brattleboro, Vermont 05301 USA 800-366-4775
Copyright © 1995 by Raymond C. Clark

# Aesop and the Athenian

STORY CARDS: AESOP'S FABLES
*compiled by Raymond C. Clark, illustrated by Hannah Bonner*
PRO LINGUA ASSOCIATES
15 Elm Street, Brattleboro, Vermont 05301 USA 800-366-4775
Copyright © 1995 by Raymond C. Clark.

# The Ants and the Grasshopper

STORY CARDS: AESOP'S FABLES
*compiled by Raymond C. Clark, illustrated by Hannah Bonner*
PRO LINGUA ASSOCIATES
15 Elm Street, Brattleboro, Vermont 05301 USA 800-366-4775
Copyright © 1995 by Raymond C. Clark.

# The Horse and the Donkey

STORY CARDS: AESOP'S FABLES
*compiled by Raymond C. Clark, illustrated by Hannah Bonner*
PRO LINGUA ASSOCIATES
15 Elm Street, Brattleboro, Vermont 05301 USA 800-366-4775
Copyright © 1995 by Raymond C. Clark.

# Aesop and the Athenian

One day a very important and serious man from Athens was walking through a village. He was going hunting with his bow and arrows. He came upon the well-known story teller, Aesop, happily playing a children's game with the village children.

"Aren't you a little old for that sort of thing," said the Athenian. "It looks rather silly for a man of your age to be acting like a child."

Aesop smiled at the man and asked him to give him his bow for a moment. Aesop loosened the bowstring and handed the unstrung bow back to the man. "If your bow is always strung tight, it will lose its spring and be useless to you. Let it be free sometimes, and it will always serve you well."

#1

# The Fox and the Grapes

One day a hungry fox saw some beautifu grapes. They were hanging in great bunches from the vine. But they were high above the ground. The fox jumped and jumped, but it could not reach them. Angrily it walked away and said, "They may look beautiful, but I am sure that they are sour inside."

#

# The Horse and the Donkey

A fat and lazy horse was traveling with a heavily loaded donkey and their owner. The donkey was sick, and its back was nearly breaking. It begged the horse to help carry the load. But the lazy horse refused.

A little farther along the road, the donkey fell down and died. The owner then threw the donkey's load on the horse's back and on top of that, the dead donkey.

#3

# The Ants and the Grasshopper

The grasshopper sang and sang all summer. But as winter came, it was not easy to find food. The grasshopper got hungry. It went to the door of its neighbors, the ants. It asked them for a little food. "I will pay you back next summer," it said.

"What did you do this summer?" asked one of the ants.

"Oh, I sang all day," answered the grasshopper.

"Well then, now you can dance," said the ant, and it closed the door.

#

## The Shepherd Boy and the Wolf

STORY CARDS: AESOP'S FABLES
*compiled by Raymond C. Clark, illustrated by Hannah Bonner*
PRO LINGUA ASSOCIATES
15 Elm Street, Brattleboro, Vermont 05301 USA 800-366-4775
Copyright © 1995 by Raymond C. Clark.

## The Rabbit and the Dog

STORY CARDS: AESOP'S FABLES
*compiled by Raymond C. Clark, illustrated by Hannah Bonner*
PRO LINGUA ASSOCIATES
15 Elm Street, Brattleboro, Vermont 05301 USA 800-366-4775
Copyright © 1995 by Raymond C. Clark.

## The Man and the Trees

STORY CARDS: AESOP'S FABLES
*compiled by Raymond C. Clark, illustrated by Hannah Bonner*
PRO LINGUA ASSOCIATES
15 Elm Street, Brattleboro, Vermont 05301 USA 800-366-4775
Copyright © 1995 by Raymond C. Clark.

## The Lion and the Fox

STORY CARDS: AESOP'S FABLES
*compiled by Raymond C. Clark, illustrated by Hannah Bonner*
PRO LINGUA ASSOCIATES
15 Elm Street, Brattleboro, Vermont 05301 USA 800-366-4775
Copyright © 1995 by Raymond C. Clark.

# The Rabbit and the Dog

A hunting dog found a fine rabbit in the field. Immediately it began to chase the rabbit. But the rabbit was an excellent runner, and in a short time the dog gave up, breathless.

The dog's master came up to the dog and teased it because it didn't catch the rabbit. "Master," said the dog, "you may laugh at me, but please remember, the rabbit was running for its life, while I was running only for your dinner."



# The Shepherd Boy and the Wolf

A young shepherd boy was bored with his work. One day he cried, "Wolf! Wolf!" to see what would happen. All the people working in the fields ran to help, but there was no wolf. The young shepherd was very pleased with all the excitement. A few days later he did it again, but the people who came were not amused.

The next day, a wolf came. The boy cried, "Wolf! Wolf!" but nobody came, and the wolf enjoyed a fine meal.



# The Lion and the Fox

A lazy lion was sitting in its den thinking about food. It thought about the wonderful meals it had enjoyed, and then it realized it had never had fox to dinner — or for dinner. So the lion sent the fox an invitation.

The fox replied. It thanked the lion for the invitation, "But I don't think I will come," it said. "I have seen many tracks leading to your den. It seems you have many visitors. But I do not see any tracks coming out."



# The Man and the Trees

One day a man came into the woods with a heavy but sharp piece of iron in his hand. He spoke to the trees and asked them to give him a stick of wood. The trees had never seen a man before, but he was small and could not do them any harm, so they gave him a nice strong branch.

The next day, the man came back with an axe head on the end of the branch and began to cut down the trees. After a little while, there were no more trees.

# The Goat and the Vine

STORY CARDS: AESOP'S FABLES
*compiled by Raymond C. Clark, illustrated by Hannah Bonner*
PRO LINGUA ASSOCIATES
15 Elm Street, Brattleboro, Vermont 05301 USA 800-366-4775
Copyright © 1995 by Raymond C. Clark.

# The Dog in the Manger

STORY CARDS: AESOP'S FABLES
*compiled by Raymond C. Clark, illustrated by Hannah Bonner*
PRO LINGUA ASSOCIATES
15 Elm Street, Brattleboro, Vermont 05301 USA 800-366-4775
Copyright © 1995 by Raymond C. Clark.

# The Lion and the Boar

STORY CARDS: AESOP'S FABLES
*compiled by Raymond C. Clark, illustrated by Hannah Bonner*
PRO LINGUA ASSOCIATES
15 Elm Street, Brattleboro, Vermont 05301 USA 800-366-4775
Copyright © 1995 by Raymond C. Clark.

# The Tortoise and the Hare

STORY CARDS: AESOP'S FABLES
*compiled by Raymond C. Clark, illustrated by Hannah Bonner*
PRO LINGUA ASSOCIATES
15 Elm Street, Brattleboro, Vermont 05301 USA 800-366-4775
Copyright © 1995 by Raymond C. Clark.

# The Dog in the Manger

A tired and hungry dog was lying in a manger. The manger was full of sweet-smelling hay. But of course, dogs do not eat hay. The manger was warm, the hay was soft, but still the dog was hungry.

A large and gentle ox came into the manger. It had been working in the fields all day long, and now it, too, was tired and hungry. It started toward the hay, but the angry dog jumped in front of the hay. It barked and snarled at the ox.

"I see, little dog in the manger," said the ox, "there is nothing here for *you* to eat, so *nobody* will eat."

#9

# The Goat and the Vine

One day, some hunters were chasing a goat. The goat hid in a thick vine and waited for the hunters to go past. After some time, the goat decided that the hunters had gone. Feeling hungry, it decided to have some lunch, and it started to eat the vine.

The goat did not realize, however, that the hunters had also decided to stop for lunch, and they were not far away. The hunters heard the rustling of the vine's leaves. Quickly, they returned and saw the vine's branches moving. Then they saw the goat and shot the ungrateful animal with their arrows.

#1

# The Tortoise and the Hare

The hare loved to tease the tortoise about its slowness. One day, the tortoise challenged the hare to a race. The hare thought this was very funny, but it agreed. The race began. Immediately, the hare raced far ahead of the tortoise. The hare decided to rest under a tree and let the tortoise catch up.

In a little while, the hare fell asleep under the tree. Time passed, and the hare woke up. It was almost dark! The hare raced to the finish line, but too late! There was the tortoise, waiting and smiling.

#11

# The Lion and the Boar

On a very hot day, a lion and a boar went to the water hole for a drink. When they saw each other, they began to argue over the water.

"I was here first," said the boar.

"I am the king," said the lion.

They were about to fight each other. Just then, they looked up in the sky and saw buzzards coming from every direction. They were beginning to circle overhead.

"I think it is better to share," said the lion.

"I think so, too," replied the boar.

#12

# The Wind and the Sun

STORY CARDS: AESOP'S FABLES
*compiled by Raymond C. Clark, illustrated by Hannah Bonner*
PRO LINGUA ASSOCIATES
15 Elm Street, Brattleboro, Vermont 05301 USA 800-366-4775
Copyright © 1995 by Raymond C. Clark.

# The Lion and the Gnat

STORY CARDS: AESOP'S FABLES
*compiled by Raymond C. Clark, illustrated by Hannah Bonner*
PRO LINGUA ASSOCIATES
15 Elm Street, Brattleboro, Vermont 05301 USA 800-366-4775
Copyright © 1995 by Raymond C. Clark.

# The Wolf in Sheep's Clothing

STORY CARDS: AESOP'S FABLES
*compiled by Raymond C. Clark, illustrated by Hannah Bonner*
PRO LINGUA ASSOCIATES
15 Elm Street, Brattleboro, Vermont 05301 USA 800-366-4775
Copyright © 1995 by Raymond C. Clark.

# The Wolf and the Lamb

STORY CARDS: AESOP'S FABLES
*compiled by Raymond C. Clark, illustrated by Hannah Bonner*
PRO LINGUA ASSOCIATES
15 Elm Street, Brattleboro, Vermont 05301 USA 800-366-4775
Copyright © 1995 by Raymond C. Clark.

# The Lion and the Gnat

A little gnat found King Lion napping under a tree. The gnat landed on the tip of the lion's nose and took a bite. The lion woke up and angrily tried to swat the gnat, but the little creature flew to the lion's back and took another bite. The lion snapped and slapped, but the gnat found another spot and bit again.

Within a few minutes the angry lion gave up the fight and ran away. The little gnat was very pleased with itself. "Wait till I tell my friends that I have defeated King Lion," it said to itself. It buzzed around and around in crazy, happy circles and flew off straight into a spider's web.

#13

# The Wind and the Sun

The wind and the sun had an argument about who was stronger. Then they saw a man walking down a road, and the sun said, "I know how to settle this argument. Let's see who can force this man to take off his coat. You can begin."

The sun hid behind a cloud and the wind began to blow and blow. But the harder it blew, the more the man pulled his coat tighter. Finally, the wind gave up.

Then the sun took its turn. It came from behind the clouds and smiled down upon the man. Within a few minutes, the man took off his coat because of the sun's warmth.

#14

# The Wolf and the Lamb

A wolf was chasing a young lamb. The poor lamb realized it could not escape, so it turned to the wolf and said, "Please, Wolf, I know I am about to die, but before you eat me, would you do me a great favor. I have heard you are a wonderful flute player. Please play for me, and I can have one last dance."

The wolf quickly agreed because it also thought it was a great flute player. It played and the lamb danced, but the shepherd's dogs heard the sound of the flute and came after the wolf. As the wolf escaped, it said to itself, "My purpose was to be a butcher, not a musician."

#15

# The Wolf in Sheep's Clothing

One day a wolf put on the skin of a sheep and crept into the middle of a flock. The sheep did not notice . The wolf had a plan. Now it could walk around in the middle of the flock and carefully choose the finest young lamb for its lunch.

Finally, the wolf made a decision and started to creep toward a young, fat lamb that looked tender and sweet. At the same time, the shepherd was preparing for his lunch. The fire was ready. The shepherd moved into the middle of the flock and quickly grabbed his lunch and killed it. He was surprised to find that underneath the sheepskin was the clever wolf.

#16

# The Bundle of Sticks

STORY CARDS: AESOP'S FABLES
*compiled by Raymond C. Clark, illustrated by Hannah Bonner*
PRO LINGUA ASSOCIATES
15 Elm Street, Brattleboro, Vermont 05301 USA 800-366-4775
Copyright © 1995 by Raymond C. Clark.

# The Rabbits and the Frogs

STORY CARDS: AESOP'S FABLES
*compiled by Raymond C. Clark, illustrated by Hannah Bonner*
PRO LINGUA ASSOCIATES
15 Elm Street, Brattleboro, Vermont 05301 USA 800-366-4775
Copyright © 1995 by Raymond C. Clark.

# The Milkmaid and Her Pail

STORY CARDS: AESOP'S FABLES
*compiled by Raymond C. Clark, illustrated by Hannah Bonner*
PRO LINGUA ASSOCIATES
15 Elm Street, Brattleboro, Vermont 05301 USA 800-366-4775
Copyright © 1995 by Raymond C. Clark.

# The Farmer and His Sons

STORY CARDS: AESOP'S FABLES
*compiled by Raymond C. Clark, illustrated by Hannah Bonner*
PRO LINGUA ASSOCIATES
15 Elm Street, Brattleboro, Vermont 05301 USA 800-366-4775
Copyright © 1995 by Raymond C. Clark.

# The Rabbits and the Frogs

Once upon a time the rabbits had a meeting. They were very tired of being afraid. They were tired of running away from all the other animals. They decided to do something. One rabbit suggested that life was not worth living. "Let's all go to the lake. We will jump in together and drown ourselves. Then our troubles will be over."

So they ran toward the lake. Just as they reached the shore, all the frogs on the shoreline jumped into the water because of the noise made by the rabbits. One of the older rabbits turned to its friends and said, "Let's think about this some more, my friends, because it seems the frogs are afraid of us."

#17

# The Bundle of Sticks

An old man became very sick. He realized that he was about to die, and he began to think about what his sons would do with his farm and all his property.

He asked one of his servants to bring him six sticks tied together into a bundle. Then he called for his six sons. He asked each of his sons, one by one, to break the bundle. None of them could do it.

Then he spoke to the oldest son and said, "Untie the bundle." Next, he told his sons to each take one stick, and then he said, "All right, now break your sticks." Each son easily broke his stick.

"I think my meaning is clear," he said.

#1

# The Farmer and His Sons

A farmer worked hard all his life to grow grapes in his vineyard. However, his sons were not very interested in farming and did not work very hard. When the farmer realized he was going to die, he called his sons together and said to them, "Before I die, I must tell you that I have buried a wonderful treasure in the vineyard. After my death you may have it."

He died in the spring, and the sons immediately started digging. They dug everywhere, but they found nothing. However, because of their digging and turning the soil over and over, there was a wonderful crop of grapes in the fall, and the sons sold the grapes for a great profit.

#19

# The Milkmaid and Her Pail

A milkmaid was going to the market carrying a pail of milk on her head. As she walked along, she began to think of what she could do with the money she got from selling the milk.

"I'll buy some chickens," she thought, "and they will lay eggs every morning. And then I will sell the eggs, and when I have enough money, I will buy a new dress and hat. And then when I go to the market, the boys will all notice me, and the other girls will be so jealous. But I won't care, I will just look at them like this, and toss my head in the air and go my way." But just as she said this, she tossed her head back and the pail and all the milk spilled to the ground.

#2

# The Goose and the Golden Egg

STORY CARDS: AESOP'S FABLES
*compiled by Raymond C. Clark, illustrated by Hannah Bonner*
PRO LINGUA ASSOCIATES
15 Elm Street, Brattleboro, Vermont 05301 USA 800-366-4775
Copyright © 1995 by Raymond C. Clark.

# The Fox and the Crow

STORY CARDS: AESOP'S FABLES
*compiled by Raymond C. Clark, illustrated by Hannah Bonner*
PRO LINGUA ASSOCIATES
15 Elm Street, Brattleboro, Vermont 05301 USA 800-366-4775
Copyright © 1995 by Raymond C. Clark.

# The Wolf and the Crane

STORY CARDS: AESOP'S FABLES
*compiled by Raymond C. Clark, illustrated by Hannah Bonner*
PRO LINGUA ASSOCIATES
15 Elm Street, Brattleboro, Vermont 05301 USA 800-366-4775
Copyright © 1995 by Raymond C. Clark.

# The Wolf and the Goat

STORY CARDS: AESOP'S FABLES
*compiled by Raymond C. Clark, illustrated by Hannah Bonner*
PRO LINGUA ASSOCIATES
15 Elm Street, Brattleboro, Vermont 05301 USA 800-366-4775
Copyright © 1995 by Raymond C. Clark.

# The Fox and the Crow

A hungry fox was walking through the woods. It saw a crow sitting in a tree enjoying a fine breakfast.

"Ah, my dear Crow," said the fox, "What a beautiful animal you are. I can see that your body, your feathers, and your color are all wonderful. I only wish I could hear your beautiful voice."

The crow felt very proud. It opened its mouth and sang in its loudest voice — which was really very ugly. But at the same time, its breakfast fell from its mouth to the mouth of the fox, who was waiting under the tree.

"You tricked me," said the crow angrily.

"Remember something," said the fox. "I said many things about your beauty, but I never said anything about your brains."

#21

# The Goose and the Golden Egg

One day a farmer was collecting eggs from the nests of his geese. In one of the nests he found a heavy, yellow egg. He took it home and tried to break it open, but it would not break. He took it to the market, where he learned that it was gold.

The next day, the same thing happened, but he observed very carefully and saw which goose had laid the egg. For the next several days, this wonderful goose continued to produce golden eggs, and the farmer sold them, becoming richer and richer.

However, as he steadily grew rich, he became greedy, and he thought that if he could get all the eggs inside the goose in one day, he could then retire and never work again. So, he killed the goose and opened it up, only to find nothing.

#2

# The Wolf and the Goat

A wolf had hunted all day long, but had found nothing. At last it saw an old goat at the top of a very steep cliff. The goat was old, and probably its meat was very tough, but it would be better than nothing.

"But how can I get it?" thought the wolf. "If I start to climb the cliff, the goat can very easily run away." Then the wolf got an idea. "Goat! Come on down here. It's much safer and the grass is much greener and tastier."

The goat, however, was old because it was also wise, and it understood the wolf's purpose. "Thanks very much for your suggestion," said the goat, "but I think I'll stay here. I'm afraid it is *your* dinner that you are thinking about, not mine."

#23

# The Wolf and the Crane

A wolf was eating its dinner one day, when a piece of bone got stuck in its throat. It was quite painful, and so it went to its friends for help. It said, " I will give anything to anyone who helps me."

No one could help the wolf. So the wolf ran to the shore of a pond and found a crane, fishing for frogs. It begged the crane to help, and at last the crane agreed to try.

The wolf opened its mouth wide and the crane put its long beak and neck into the wolf's mouth. The crane found the piece of bone and carefully removed it from the wolf's throat.

"Now, what is my reward?" asked the crane.

The wolf grinned and said, "You put your head inside a wolf's mouth and you still have your head. *That* is your reward."

#2

# The Blind Man and the Lame Man

STORY CARDS: AESOP'S FABLES
*compiled by Raymond C. Clark, illustrated by Hannah Bonner*
PRO LINGUA ASSOCIATES
15 Elm Street, Brattleboro, Vermont 05301 USA 800-366-4775
Copyright © 1995 by Raymond C. Clark.

# The Fox and the Stork

STORY CARDS: AESOP'S FABLES
*compiled by Raymond C. Clark, illustrated by Hannah Bonner*
PRO LINGUA ASSOCIATES
15 Elm Street, Brattleboro, Vermont 05301 USA 800-366-4775
Copyright © 1995 by Raymond C. Clark.

# The Mice and the Cat

STORY CARDS: AESOP'S FABLES
*compiled by Raymond C. Clark, illustrated by Hannah Bonner*
PRO LINGUA ASSOCIATES
15 Elm Street, Brattleboro, Vermont 05301 USA 800-366-4775
Copyright © 1995 by Raymond C. Clark.

# The Men and the Oyster

STORY CARDS: AESOP'S FABLES
*compiled by Raymond C. Clark, illustrated by Hannah Bonner*
PRO LINGUA ASSOCIATES
15 Elm Street, Brattleboro, Vermont 05301 USA 800-366-4775
Copyright © 1995 by Raymond C. Clark.

# The Fox and the Stork

One day a fox invited its friend, a stork, to come to its house for dinner. The fox cooked a delicious soup, but it decided to play a trick on its friend. It served the soup in a flat dish so the stork could only sip a little at a time with its long pointed beak. Meanwhile, the fox quickly lapped up the soup with its tongue. The polite, but angry, stork thanked the fox and went home.

A little while later, the fox received an invitation from the stork. The stork prepared a nice dish of chopped meat. The smell filled the room, and the fox could not wait to begin. The stork served the dinner in a tall pot with a narrow mouth. The stork easily stuck its long beak into the pot and pulled out piece after piece of the meat. The fox with its shorter nose could not reach the food in the pot, but the fox understood the stork's trick, smiled and went home hungry.

#25

# The Blind Man and the Lame Man

At a very rough stretch of road, a blind man continued to stumble and fall. Exhausted, he finally sat down in despair in the middle of the road. Not long after, a man with only one good leg reached the same place in the road and saw the blind man.

"Why are you sitting there?" asked the lame man.

"This road is too much for me," sighed the blind man. "I cannot see all the bumps and ruts. Do you think you could help me?"

"Not likely," said the lame man. "My one good leg is barely enough to keep me on my feet. But it appears that your legs are strong. If you will carry me upon your shoulders, I will be your eyes, and you will be my legs. Together we can succeed."

In this way, the two travelers went along safely to the next town. In fact, they continued to travel together for many years.

#2

# The Men and the Oyster

Two men were walking along the seaside. They saw an oyster, and they both reached for it at the same time. One pushed the other, and very soon they were in a heated argument. They both wanted the oyster.

Another man came walking along, and they stopped him. "Will you please be a judge for us. Listen to our stories and decide who is right."

The man agreed and asked them to let him hold the oyster. He listened to their stories, but before they finished with their arguments and counter-arguments, the man took out his knife and opened the oyster. When they were finished, he swallowed the oyster and handed each of them a half-shell. "The court gives each of you a shell. The oyster will cover the court's costs."

#27

# The Mice and the Cat

Everybody knows that mice are very afraid of cats. Many years ago, the mice tried to solve this problem. They had a big meeting to find ways to defeat their great enemy, the cat.

Many mice spoke at the meeting. Many ideas were given, but none of them seemed very good. Finally, one young mouse spoke up in a loud voice. "I have a great idea," it said. "You all know that the cat creeps up very silently, and we don't know it is coming. I suggest that we put a bell around the cat's neck so that we can hear it as it moves."

The mice were very excited by this idea. "Let's do it!" they said.

Just then, one of the older mice spoke up and said, "This is all very well, but who is going to put the bell around the cat's neck?"

Nobody spoke up.

#2

# The Travelers and the Bear

STORY CARDS: AESOP'S FABLES
*compiled by Raymond C. Clark, illustrated by Hannah Bonner*
PRO LINGUA ASSOCIATES
15 Elm Street, Brattleboro, Vermont 05301 USA 800-366-4775
Copyright © 1995 by Raymond C. Clark.

# The Stork and the Farmer

STORY CARDS: AESOP'S FABLES
*compiled by Raymond C. Clark, illustrated by Hannah Bonner*
PRO LINGUA ASSOCIATES
15 Elm Street, Brattleboro, Vermont 05301 USA 800-366-4775
Copyright © 1995 by Raymond C. Clark.

# The Dog and the Donkey

STORY CARDS: AESOP'S FABLES
*compiled by Raymond C. Clark, illustrated by Hannah Bonner*
PRO LINGUA ASSOCIATES
15 Elm Street, Brattleboro, Vermont 05301 USA 800-366-4775
Copyright © 1995 by Raymond C. Clark.

# The Bee and the Fly

STORY CARDS: AESOP'S FABLES
*compiled by Raymond C. Clark, illustrated by Hannah Bonner*
PRO LINGUA ASSOCIATES
15 Elm Street, Brattleboro, Vermont 05301 USA 800-366-4775
Copyright © 1995 by Raymond C. Clark.

# The Stork and the Farmer

A flock of cranes invited a stork to go to a party. "We're going to the farmer's field," one of them said. "He has just finished planting his crops, and we'll have a lot of fun and good food." The stork didn't get many invitations to parties, so it accepted.

The unfortunate birds did not realize that the farmer had hidden a net on the field. One by one, they all got their feet tangled in the net.

Then the farmer appeared. The stork called to the farmer, "Oh, sir, please let me go. You can see I am a stork, and I do not belong to this group of thieves. I only came here for fun. I didn't know they would try to eat your crops."

"I see that you are a stork," the farmer said. "But I caught you with thieves, and you will be treated as a thief."

#29

# The Bee and the Fly

A bee, sitting atop its hive noticed a fly hanging around. With an angry buzz, it said to the fly, "What are you flitting around here for? Don't you know this is the home of the noble and busy bees?"

"Oh, really? What makes you so special, and why are you so angry?" asked the fly.

"We bees have the best laws and the best government. We feed upon nature's beautiful flowers, and we produce nature's sweetest food, honey. And you, you miserable thing, have nothing, and you eat the most horrible things in the world."

"I may be poor," said the fly, "but my heart is free and sweet while yours is bitter. Why, you are so full of hate that if anyone comes near, you inject them with your anger, and revenge is so strong in you that you are ready to die, just so you can sting. I'll be happy to go away and enjoy my simple life."

#31

# The Travelers and the Bear

Two travelers were on their way through a forest when they met a bear. The bear growled and started after them. There was a tree with some low branches near the men. One of the men started climbing the tree without looking back or helping his companion. The other man did not have time to follow. He fell at the foot of the tree, held his breath, and lay still.

The bear came up to the man lying on th ground and sniffed at him, but it thought the man was dead. It went away.

The other man come down from the tree and said to his companion, "I saw the bear whisper something in your ear. What did it say?"

"The bear said, 'In times of danger, you find out who your real friends are'," replied the other traveler.

#3

# The Dog and the Donkey

A man, his donkey, and a dog were traveling The man decided to take a break, and he fel asleep under a tree by the side of the road. The donkey wandered out into the field, feeding on the grass. As soon as they were some distance away from the man, the dog said something quietly to the donkey.

"You're having a nice lunch, but I'm quite hungry. If you would only lie down for a moment or two, I could reach into the pack that you're carrying and have a bite or two of food."

The donkey was not interested in helping the dog. "You'll just have to wait until the master wakes up. He'll give you some food."

Suddenly, a wolf sprang out from behind a tree and grabbed the donkey by the neck. "Help! Help!" cried the donkey to the dog.

The dog, however, would not move. "You'll just have to wait until the master wakes up. He'll help you," said the dog.

#3

# The Travelers and the Purse

STORY CARDS: AESOP'S FABLES
*compiled by Raymond C. Clark, illustrated by Hannah Bonner*
PRO LINGUA ASSOCIATES
15 Elm Street, Brattleboro, Vermont 05301 USA 800-366-4775
Copyright © 1995 by Raymond C. Clark.

# The Lion's Tax

STORY CARDS: AESOP'S FABLES
*compiled by Raymond C. Clark, illustrated by Hannah Bonner*
PRO LINGUA ASSOCIATES
15 Elm Street, Brattleboro, Vermont 05301 USA 800-366-4775
Copyright © 1995 by Raymond C. Clark.

# The Lion, the Fox, and the Donkey

STORY CARDS: AESOP'S FABLES
*compiled by Raymond C. Clark, illustrated by Hannah Bonner*
PRO LINGUA ASSOCIATES
15 Elm Street, Brattleboro, Vermont 05301 USA 800-366-4775
Copyright © 1995 by Raymond C. Clark.

# The Lion and the Mouse

STORY CARDS: AESOP'S FABLES
*compiled by Raymond C. Clark, illustrated by Hannah Bonner*
PRO LINGUA ASSOCIATES
15 Elm Street, Brattleboro, Vermont 05301 USA 800-366-4775
Copyright © 1995 by Raymond C. Clark.

# The Lion's Tax

A lion was growing tired of hunting, and it decided that all the other animals should give it a share of their food, like a tax. Then it could retire and never be hungry. So the lion went to its advisors to decide on the form of the tax.

The tiger gave its opinion. "The best tax should be based on each animal's vices. For example, if an animal did something wrong, it would have to pay a fine. That will raise taxes and make our world a little better."

"No!" said the elephant, "that will never work. Nobody will admit to wrongdoing. Then we will have to go to court and hire lawyers, and in the end, we will never collect any tax. I have a better idea. We will tax everyone according to their virtues. Each animal will simply decide how virtuous it is and pay accordingly. Who would refuse to pay something?"

#33

# The Travelers and the Purse

Two men were traveling together when one of them saw a purse by the side of the road. He picked it up and looked inside to discove that it was full of money. "Look what *I* have found!" he cried.

"Ah, but we are traveling together," said the other man. "You should say, 'look what *we* have found'."

"Why should I?" said the first man. "*I* found it, and *I* should keep it for myself." H put the money into his pocket and tossed th purse back to the roadside.

Just then they heard a lot of noise behin them and a shout, "Look! They have the purse. Stop, thieves." The two men turned to see an angry mob coming toward them.

"Oh, no! They will think we stole it," sai the first man.

"*We*?" said the second man. "I believe '*your*' money is in *your* pocket."

#

# The Lion and the Mouse

Once a little mouse was busily searching for food. It was running up and down and around a sleeping lion looking for scraps. Suddenly, the lion woke up . The king of beasts grabbed the tiny mouse in its huge paw. The lion was about to swallow the poor mouse when the mouse said, "Please, let me go and I will do something for you some day."

The lion was amused. "I don't know how *you* can help *me*," it said, "But I am not so hungry, you are only a tiny mouthful, and you have amused me." And the lion let the little mouse escape.

Some time after that, the lion became caught in a trap made of ropes. It roared and struggled, but it could not escape. The little mouse heard the lion's frightened roar and came to help. It saw the lion trapped in the ropes, and it busily went to work. It chewed on the ropes until the lion broke free from the trap and escaped. Forever after, the lion and the mouse often had lunch together.

#35

# The Lion, the Fox, and the Donkey

A lion, a fox and a donkey went hunting together. They agreed that whatever they caugh would be shared among them. After a while, th donkey heard a deer in the woods, the fox followe it with its sensitive nose, and the lion killed it.

The lion then told the donkey to divide the deer, and the donkey carefully cut it up into three equal pieces. When the lion came to eat it saw what the donkey had done and it was enraged.

"As king of the beasts, I deserve the largest share," and with a roar it jumped upon the poo donkey and killed it on the spot. "Now you divide the dinner," said the lion to the fox.

The fox took a small bite and then turned to the lion. "The rest is yours," it said.

The lion was pleased and asked the fox how it had learned to show respect.

"To tell the truth," said the fox, "The donkey taught me."

#

# The Men and the Chameleon

STORY CARDS: AESOP'S FABLES
*compiled by Raymond C. Clark, illustrated by Hannah Bonner*
PRO LINGUA ASSOCIATES
15 Elm Street, Brattleboro, Vermont 05301 USA 800-366-4775
Copyright © 1995 by Raymond C. Clark.

# The Man and the Nightingale

STORY CARDS: AESOP'S FABLES
*compiled by Raymond C. Clark, illustrated by Hannah Bonner*
PRO LINGUA ASSOCIATES
15 Elm Street, Brattleboro, Vermont 05301 USA 800-366-4775
Copyright © 1995 by Raymond C. Clark.

# Androcles and the Lion

STORY CARDS: AESOP'S FABLES
*compiled by Raymond C. Clark, illustrated by Hannah Bonner*
PRO LINGUA ASSOCIATES
15 Elm Street, Brattleboro, Vermont 05301 USA 800-366-4775
Copyright © 1995 by Raymond C. Clark.

# The Salt Peddler and the Donkey

STORY CARDS: AESOP'S FABLES
*compiled by Raymond C. Clark, illustrated by Hannah Bonner*
PRO LINGUA ASSOCIATES
15 Elm Street, Brattleboro, Vermont 05301 USA 800-366-4775
Copyright © 1995 by Raymond C. Clark.

# The Man and the Nightingale

One night a man lay awake in his bed listening to the wonderful song of the nightingale. The man decided that he would trap the nightingale, and then it could never fly away. It would sing for him every night.

The next day he built a trap, and in the night he captured the nightingale. "Now you will always sing for me," said the man.

"Nightingales never sing in a cage," said the bird.

"Then I will eat you," said the man.

"Wait!" said the nightingale. "If you let me go, I will tell you three things that are worth much more than my poor body." The man let the bird loose and it flew to a branch in a tree, where it looked down on the man.

Then the bird said to the man, "Here are my three things: First, never believe the promise of a captive. Second, keep what you have, and third, do not cry over what is gone forever." And it flew away.

#37

# The Men and the Chameleon

Three hunters came to Samos for hunting and hired Aesop to be their guide. During the day, they went off in different directions and each o them saw a chameleon, an animal they had never seen before.

That evening, after the hunt, they all told of the strange animal they had seen. The first on said, it was brown. The second one argued fiercely, saying it was green, and the third one said, "Both of you are wrong. It is black, and t prove it, I caught one and put it in my bag," — which happened to be white.

The third man pulled the chameleon from h bag, and it was white! The three men were amazed. And then Aesop told them about the chameleon's ability to change color.

"So you see," said Aesop, "How we each vie the world from our own experience. Each of yo had some of the truth, but none of you had all the truth."

#

# The Salt Peddler and the Donkey

A salt peddler bought a new donkey to carry salt from the seashore to the mountains, where he sold it. Day after day he traveled to the seashore and back up the steep mountain trail. The donkey did not mind going down to the cool seashore, but it hated the trip back.

One day, the donkey stumbled as it crossed the river, and fell into the water. After the peddler pulled it out, they continued, but the river water had dissolved part of the donkey's load of salt, and it was much lighter.

The clever donkey then began to fall into the river on every trip. Of course, the peddler was losing salt and his profit.

The peddler got an idea. One day, he bought sponges instead of salt. The donkey fell into the river as usual, but this time, it had to carry a load of wet sponges up the mountain path. After that, the donkey crossed the river safely.

#39

# Androcles and the Lion

A slave named Androcles escaped from his master and went to live in the forest. One day he wa walking in the forest when he saw a lion. The lion roared, and Androcles started to run away, but he saw that the lion was in pain. Carefully, Androcles approached the lion and asked it wha was wrong. The lion showed him its paw with a large thorn in it.

"I'll take it out," said Androcles, "but please don't hurt me."

"I promise," said the lion, and then Androcles carefully removed the thorn. The lion thanked him and Androcles went away.

A little while after that, Androcles was recapture He was put in jail, and then one afternoon he wa taken to the arena. As he walked into the middl of the arena he saw a hungry lion coming towar him. Androcles waited in fear. But the lion stopped just in front of Androcles and happily licked his face. It was the same lion that Androcles had helped in the forest. Everyone in the arena was amazed, and the emperor was so pleased to see this incredible sight that he let them both go back to live in the forest.

#

# The Donkey and the Horse

STORY CARDS: AESOP'S FABLES
*compiled by Raymond C. Clark, illustrated by Hannah Bonner*
PRO LINGUA ASSOCIATES
15 Elm Street, Brattleboro, Vermont 05301 USA 800-366-4775
Copyright © 1995 by Raymond C. Clark.

# The Young Mouse, the Cat, and the Rooster

STORY CARDS: AESOP'S FABLES
*compiled by Raymond C. Clark, illustrated by Hannah Bonner*
PRO LINGUA ASSOCIATES
15 Elm Street, Brattleboro, Vermont 05301 USA 800-366-4775
Copyright © 1995 by Raymond C. Clark.

# The Fox, the Rooster, and the Dog

STORY CARDS: AESOP'S FABLES
*compiled by Raymond C. Clark, illustrated by Hannah Bonner*
PRO LINGUA ASSOCIATES
15 Elm Street, Brattleboro, Vermont 05301 USA 800-366-4775
Copyright © 1995 by Raymond C. Clark.

# The Fox and the Goat

STORY CARDS: AESOP'S FABLES
*compiled by Raymond C. Clark, illustrated by Hannah Bonner*
PRO LINGUA ASSOCIATES
15 Elm Street, Brattleboro, Vermont 05301 USA 800-366-4775
Copyright © 1995 by Raymond C. Clark.

# The Young Mouse, the Cat, and the Rooster

One day a young mouse decided to explore the world beyond its nest. When its mother wasn't looking, it sneaked outside. It looked across the yard and saw a large furry animal with a long tail. The animal was sitting peacefully in the sun. It smiled and smiled and made the nicest purring sound. The little mouse began to walk across the yard to introduce itself to this handsome animal when it saw a tall and ugly monster furiously scratching the earth. Quickly, it ran back to its nest.

"And where have you been?" asked the mouse's mother.

"Oh, mother, I was just going to meet a smiling and furry new friend when a horrible monster came along. It had only two legs. It was very tall. It had strange red things on its head. Its mouth was like a spear and it made the most awful noise."

"My child," said the mouse's mother. "You were very lucky. Your 'monster' is the barnyard rooster, who doesn't bother us at all. Your 'friend' is the cat, who eats us."

#41

# The Donkey and the Horse

A donkey and a horse were traveling along togethe in the company of their master, who was travelin on some important business for the king. The horse was dressed in beautiful colors. It had a wonderful leather saddle and a fine harness. Tl master rode on the proud horse's back with a shiny sword hanging from his belt.

The poor donkey, however, stumbled along with a heavy load in worn and dirty baskets on i back. When they came to a resting place, the donkey spoke to the horse. "I wish I were you," i sighed. "Your life is so glamorous, and mine is s dull and boring."

The next day, the horse and master rode over the hill and left the donkey behind. There was a great noise from beyond the hill. It continued all afternoon, and then it stopped. The donkey waitec patiently, but its master and the horse did not return. Finally, the donkey walked to the top of tl hill and looked down upon a great battleground where the horse lay dead beside its fallen master.

"It's not so bad to be a donkey," it said to itsel as it turned to go back home.

#

# The Fox and the Goat

One day a fox was chasing a bird through a field when it fell into a well. Fortunately, the well was not very deep, and there was not much water in the bottom of the well. The fox tried to jump out, but the well was just a little too deep. The fox was stuck.

In a little while, the fox heard the tinkling bells of some goats, and the fox started thinking. One of the goats came near the well, and the fox cried out, "Go away!" Curious, the goat looked down into the well and saw the fox.

"What are you doing there?" asked the goat.

"Haven't you heard?" asked the fox. "There is a great drought coming, and I jumped down here so I will have water. But there's enough for two if you want to jump in."

The foolish goat jumped in, and as it did so, the fox jumped on the goat's back and jumped out of the well.

"Where are you going?" cried the goat.

"Oh, don't worry, I'll come back when the drought comes," said the fox as it ran away.

#43

# The Fox, the Rooster, and the Dog

One evening a fox was sneaking around the barnyard. It saw a fat rooster up in the branche of a tree, beyond its reach. "I have some very good news," said the fox.

"What is it?" asked the rooster.

The fox answered, "King Lion has announcec that there will be peace in the animal kingdom. No animal may hurt another, and we will all liv in peace. Isn't that wonderful? Come on down, and I will tell you more."

"That is good news," said the rooster, as it looked across the field. "I'll be down in a moment, and we can share this good news with someone else who is coming toward us."

"Oh? Who do you see?" asked the fox.

The rooster smiled to itself and said, "It's onl the farmer's dog, running toward us."

Suddenly, the fox began to run away. "Wher are you going?" asked the rooster. "Don't you want to share the news with the dog?"

"I would," said the fox, "but it might not believe me."

# The City Mouse and the Country Mouse

STORY CARDS: AESOP'S FABLES
*compiled by Raymond C. Clark, illustrated by Hannah Bonner*
PRO LINGUA ASSOCIATES
15 Elm Street, Brattleboro, Vermont 05301 USA 800-366-4775
Copyright © 1995 by Raymond C. Clark.

# The Miser

STORY CARDS: AESOP'S FABLES
*compiled by Raymond C. Clark, illustrated by Hannah Bonner*
PRO LINGUA ASSOCIATES
15 Elm Street, Brattleboro, Vermont 05301 USA 800-366-4775
Copyright © 1995 by Raymond C. Clark.

# The Wolf and the Dog

STORY CARDS: AESOP'S FABLES
*compiled by Raymond C. Clark, illustrated by Hannah Bonner*
PRO LINGUA ASSOCIATES
15 Elm Street, Brattleboro, Vermont 05301 USA 800-366-4775
Copyright © 1995 by Raymond C. Clark.

# The Donkey's Brains

STORY CARDS: AESOP'S FABLES
*compiled by Raymond C. Clark, illustrated by Hannah Bonner*
PRO LINGUA ASSOCIATES
15 Elm Street, Brattleboro, Vermont 05301 USA 800-366-4775
Copyright © 1995 by Raymond C. Clark.

# The Miser

There was a man who loved money more than anything else in the world. He hated to spend it. He was also afraid of losing it or having it stolen by thieves. One day he decided to change all his money into gold. But still he was afraid that somebody would find it, and so he buried it in his garden.

Every two or three days he would go out to his garden and dig up the gold so he could look at it. Then he would bury it again because he never intended to spend it. One day, he came out to the garden to discover that somebody had learned about his secret. His gold was gone. He moaned and groaned and screamed and cried until his neighbor came running to see what had happened.

Finally, the miser settled down and told his neighbor about his buried gold. His neighbor smiled and said to him. "You really haven't lost anything. Just bury a big rock and pretend it is gold. Since you never planned to spend it anyway, the rock will be as good as gold for you, and you can dig it up and bury it anytime you want to."

#45

# The City Mouse and the Country Mouse

One day, the city mouse went to visit its country cousin. The country mouse was very pleased to have its city cousin visit, and it gave its cousin the very best food — beans, cheese and bread. But the city cousin turned up its nose and said, "My poor cousin, how simply you eat and live. Come to the city with me to see the good life." So the two of them set off for the bright lights of the city.

They arrived in the evening, and immediately the city mouse took its country cousin to the dining room in the great house where it lived. The room was empty, but the table was loaded with leftovers. The two mice busily sampled the cakes and jams and all the other fine foods.

Suddenly, as they were eating, the door opened and in came the servants with two huge dogs to clear the tables and eat the scraps. The mice barely escaped through a hole in the wall. The country mouse immediately asked its city cousin to show it the way home.

"Why are you going home so soon?" asked the city mouse.

The country mouse answered, "Beans and bread in peace are better than cakes and ale in fear."

#

# The Donkey's Brains

One day the fox and the lion were hunting together. They were not successful. In fact, the hunting had been very poor for several days. They were resting when the fox said to the lion, "I have an idea. You, as king of the beasts, should send a message to the donkey. You should invite it to join the royal family and become a prince of the beasts."

The donkey received the invitation with great pleasure and went immediately to the lion's den. The lion and the fox were waiting, of course, and the lion jumped on the poor donkey and killed it.

"Before we start eating," said the lion, "I have to get the rest of my family. You stay here and guard our dinner, but don't you dare take one bite until I return."

The fox waited, but it was too hungry, and it ate up the donkey's brains. When the lion came back with its family, it was very angry to see that the fox had already eaten the brains, the lion's favorite food. "How dare you eat the brains," said the angry lion. "I told you to wait."

"Brains?" said the fox. "It had no brains. If it had had any brains, it wouldn't have accepted the invitation."

#47

# The Wolf and the Dog

One day a hungry wolf was on its way home after another unsuccessful day of hunting. It met a strong and healthy dog on the way.

The dog looked at the wolf with pity. "You certainly have a hard life," said the dog. "You should come and live with me. I have lots of food every day and I really don't have to work very hard for it."

"What do you do?" asked the wolf.

"Not much, really, I just watch the master's house and keep away the thieves. It's an easy job," said the dog.

"I could do that," said the wolf, and it decided to go along with the dog. But as they were trotting along together toward town, the wolf noticed a bald spot on the dog's neck. "What's wrong with your neck?" asked the wolf.

"Oh, that?" answered the dog. "That's because of the collar I have to wear when they chain me up."

"What!" exclaimed the wolf. "You mean you're not free to come and go as you please?"

"Not all the time," replied the dog. And with that, the wolf quickly turned around and ran back to the forest.

#